Navigation
Exercises
for Yachtsmen

Navigation Exercises
for Yachtsmen
Second Edition

Lt Cdr Bill Anderson
Cruising Secretary, RYA

Produced in conjunction with the
Royal Yachting Association

STANFORD MARITIME · LONDON

Stanford Maritime Limited
Member Company of the George Philip Group
12–14 Long Acre London WC2E 9LP
Editor Phoebe Mason

First published in Great Britain 1974
Second edition 1981
Copyright © William S.B. Anderson 1974, 1981

Set in Linotron 11pt Times by
Scribe Design, Gillingham, Kent
Printed in Great Britain by
J.W. Arrowsmith, Bristol

British Library Cataloguing in Publication Data

Anderson, Bill
   Navigation exercises for yachtsmen.
   – 2nd ed.
   1. Navigation – Problems, exercises, etc.
   I. Title   II. Royal Yachting Association
   623.89′076   UK145
   ISBN 0–540–07275–3

The tables for Rise and Fall of Tide, Tidal Height Differences and other
tidal data are reproduced by kind permission of *Reed's Nautical Almanac*.

Contents

Introduction

This book was first published in 1974 as a set of practice exercises for candidates for the RYA/DoT Yachtmaster Offshore certificate. Since then a number of aspects of navigation have changed, a new buoyage system has been introduced, there are many more metric charts, and there have been alterations to the form of presentation of a number of navigational tables. These changes made it necessary to revise the book but they are not the sole reason for the revision. Over the last six years several hundred candidates have failed Yachtmaster exams (several thousand have passed them as well) and the exercises have been reorganised to give greater emphasis to subjects which have been the most common causes of failures.

Accuracy

It is difficult to quantify navigational accuracy in terms of degrees or miles, but the good navigator is the one who knows the limits of accuracy to which he can work. The apparent accuracy of the answers to some of the questions in this book is not necessarily that which would be attainable in practice, but it is important to remember that errors can be cumulative as easily as self-cancelling and all avoidable errors must therefore be eliminated. If it is impossible to guarantee the accuracy of a bearing observed or a course steered to within narrower limits than plus or minus five degrees there is no reason to plot that bearing or course less accurately than possible. An error of five degrees in observing a bearing added to a five degree plotting error results in a total error of ten degrees. The plotting of bearings and courses can be carried out to an accuracy of plus or minus one degree under all but the most severe conditions and to work to broader limits is simply to build in unnecessary inaccuracies.

Introduction

In tidal calculations there are occasions when the tide will not reach the predicted height at the predicted time, but this should be accounted for by allowing a safety margin rather than by vaguely rounding off the figures in the calculation. Heights of tide seldom differ from those predicted by more than three feet, so a built-in safety margin of that amount will make a safe allowance for the inaccuracies of the predictions. Always rounding off the calculations and always rounding off on the safe side may work most of the time, but this method leaves the navigator thinking he is safe without ever knowing quite by how much.

Tables

The tables used in this book are in the same form as those published in *Reed's Nautical Almanac*. This almanac has the advantage of providing nearly all the tabular information that a yachtsman requires in a single book. The information it contains is therefore relatively cheap and easy to stow compared with the same information from equivalent Admiralty publications, which are slightly more accurate but considerably more expensive and bulky. *Reed's* is now accepted by yachtsmen as a standard set of tables because of its cheapness and conciseness.

Tidiness

Tidiness is a virtue in chartwork for two reasons. First, tidy chartwork is easy to understand and gross errors therefore become readily apparent. Second, the navigation of a yacht is often carried out by several people working in different watches and it is much easier for the oncoming watch to pick up the threads if they can see from the chart exactly what the previous watch have been doing. A standard set of symbols makes chartwork neater and easier to understand if it is used by everyone in the crew. A suggested set is shown on page 11.

Drawing instruments

Two drawing instruments are required to complete the exercises in this book, one for drawing straight lines on set bearings and one for measuring distances. There are half a dozen different instruments available for drawing straight lines: rolling rulers, stepping rulers, set-squares, square-sided protractors and various proprietary plotting instruments. For work on a large and steady table the rolling or stepping rulers are probably the most accurate and easiest to use, but before buying a long and heavy parallel ruler it is as well to consider whether or not it will be usable on a small and very unsteady chart table at sea. A little accuracy, and it need only be very little, may well be worth sacrificing in favour of the ease of use under difficult conditions at sea which one of the proprietary plotting instruments offers. For measuring distances there is no real alternative to a pair of dividers and the bow type are the easiest to use. Pencils for chartwork should be 2Bs. They make a clear mark with very little pressure and are much kinder to the charts than harder pencils.

Conventions

All times given in the questions and answers are BST (British Summer Time). It is standard navigational practice to work in local standard time and for the UK sailing season this is BST. Confusion is only likely to arise when extracting times from tide tables which are compiled in GMT. All courses and bearings in the text are marked (C) compass, (M) magnetic, or (T) true. The chartwork diagrams show courses labelled by true bearings.

Positions are given in degrees, minutes and tenths of minutes, e.g. 50° 01'.5N, 04° 54'.8W. This style of notation is that used by the Admiralty and DoT and this should be adhered to in working the examples, although in some almanacs and other publications alternative styles will be found.

Practical navigation

There is a world of difference between being a good navigator on the dining room table and being a good navigator at sea, which this book can do little to lessen. The conversion from dining room table to chart table can only be achieved by practice and experience and the beginner may be discouraged by apparently poor results when he first navigates a yacht at sea. He need not be, because accuracy is acquired quite quickly by familiarity with a particular boat, a particular crew and a particular set of navigational instruments.

If the mathematics and plotting are correct, a landfall made in an unexpected place must be due to one of the following.

Bad steering The perfect helmsman does not exist, and an honest bad helmsman is a much lesser evil than a dishonest one. The crew should be encouraged to log the course they have actually steered rather than the one they were asked to steer.

Compass error This is often caused by metal objects placed too close to the compass; some types of beer can are capable of introducing a 30° error. If there is any doubt about the overall accuracy of the compass it should be checked and swung by a qualified compass adjuster.

Log error Always compare the distance run between fixes with the distance recorded by the log. There will be discrepancies due to current or tidal streams, but if these are allowed for the error of the log can be calculated and applied.

Wrong estimate of leeway Familiarity with the boat will lead to better estimates being made.

Bad fixing Practice with the hand bearing compass and radio direction finder will improve the accuracy of fixes.

There is no substitute for experience, but to be useful experience has to be carefully analysed. It is impossible to learn from mistakes if one does not know what mistakes one has made, so if a poor landfall is made the reason must be found. If it is not the next one will be just as poor, but if it is the next will be that much closer to the target.

The final point which must be made about navigation is that lines on charts do not necessarily catch tides or make fast passages. The right lines on the charts combined with well set sails and a well maintained engine invariably do.

Standard chartwork symbols

1 Courses

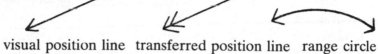

The first figures are the course made good and the second, in brackets, the course steered.

2 Position lines

visual position line   transferred position line   range circle

The arrows on position lines point away from the object observed.

3 Positions

DR   EP   fix

4 Tidal stream vectors

5 Clearing lines

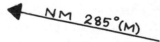

On clearing lines, the arrows point towards the object observed.

11

Part I
Navigational Facts

The following three exercises are about the basic tools of the navigator's trade: charts, man-made aids to navigation and the magnetic compass.

Charts are available from three sources, the Admiralty, publishing companies such as Stanford Maritime and Imray, Laurie, Norrie & Wilson, and foreign hydrographic offices. The British Admiralty chart has an international reputation for high standards. The series provides world wide coverage, it has the backing of the survey ships of the Royal Navy and data available through the International Hydrographic Organisation, and is supported by a comprehensive correcting service. Stanford and Imray charts are, in the main, based on Admiralty charts and their coverage is restricted to the more popular areas of Northern Europe. Admiralty charts are published on three ranges of scale: passage charts, coastal charts and harbour plans. The amount of detail which can be shown is enormous and where the best charts are required there is nothing comparable. Stanford and Imray charts are published specifically for yachtsmen and in the areas for which they are available they are a cheap and convenient alternative. Foreign charts sometimes provide more comprehensive information on the coastal waters of the country of origin.

Exercise 1 consists of questions on chart symbols and plotting positions on a chart. The need for familiarity with the symbols used on charts is too obvious to require emphasis. A complete key is published by the Admiralty as chart 5011. If you do not know the answers to any of the questions on symbols, looking them up in chart 5011 is likely to be much more instructive than simply looking them up in the answers at the back of the book. Positions in this exercise are expressed either as latitude and longitude or as a range and bearing **from** a conspicuous charted object.

Exercise 2 is about buoyage and navigational lights. The buoyage in use throughout Northern Europe is the IALA System. This is a very simple system which should allow the navigator to tell, at a glance, on which side of a buoy or beacon the safe water lies. The buoyage convention is useful but it is not designed to allow you to navigate without reference to a chart. The characteristics of a buoy allow you to make an instant appreciation of the feature it marks but that first reaction must be followed by a check with the chart. In many cases buoys are positioned for the benefit of large ships drawing 5 metres or more and it may be safer for a yacht to navigate outside rather than inside the buoyed channel, allowing large vessels unimpeded use of the deep water.

Exercise 3 consists mainly of questions on conversion between true, magnetic and compass courses and bearings. It is up to the individual to decide whether he works on the chart in true or magnetic; there are advantages and disadvantages in both. Working in magnetic reduces the number of conversions which have to be carried out but it does not eliminate them completely. Working in true is likely to be slightly more accurate but increases the number of conversions and hence the possibility of making a gross error. Whichever is chosen there is still a need for some conversions to be calculated. The sums involved are very simple but it is surprisingly easy to make a stupid mistake and add instead of subtracting. With plenty of practice, however, it should be possible to minimise these mistakes.

Exercise 1

Charts

1 Give the positions of the following, both as latitude and longitude and as a range and bearing from North Foreland Light:

Exercise 1 Charts

a North Goodwin Light Vessel (close to bottom right-hand corner of the chart).
b Tongue Light Vessel (a quarter of the way up the chart, just right of centre).
c Spaniard buoy (north of Whitstable).

2 Describe the features charted in the following positions:

a 136°(T) N Foreland Light, 1.8M.
b 025°(T) N Foreland Light, 2.2M.
c 305°(T) N Foreland Light, 6.6M.
d 51° 40′.1 N, 1° 23′.0 E.
e 51° 33′.0 N, 1° 24′.5 E.
f 51° 23′.8 N, 1° 14′.6 E.

3 On the portion of a chart below twelve of the symbols have been circled. What does each of them mean?

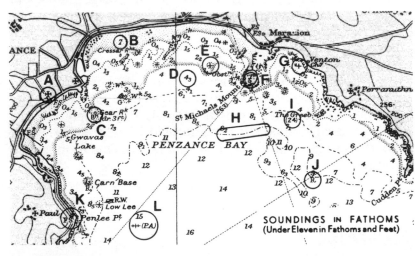

Reproduced with the sanction of the Controller, HM Stationery Office and of the Hydrographer of the Navy

4 Open your dividers the exact distance between 51° 20′N and 51° 30′ N.

a What distance does this represent on the chart at this latitude?
b Keeping your dividers open exactly the same amount, what

is the distance north from 51° 50′ N that they represent on the chart at that latitude?

c Explain why there is a difference between answers a and b. What is the general navigational significance of the difference?

5 What are the reasons for the following 'rules' of good navigational practice?

a Always use the largest scale chart available for navigation.
b Never have more than one chart spread out on the chart table at any time.
c When changing charts, always transfer the latest navigational position by two independent methods.
d Always use a 2B pencil for chartwork.
e Never rub out chartwork on a wet chart.
f Always use conventional symbols for chartwork.
Can there ever be any reason to disregard these rules?

6 What are the relative advantages of the following pairs of publications?

a Admiralty List of Lights and a yachtsman's almanac.
b Admiralty Sailing Directions and sailing directions or 'pilot books' for yachtsmen produced by commercial publishers.

7 What is the most convenient form in which yachtsmen can obtain information on changes to charts?

8 What is the most complete and concise source of radio information for small craft in Northern Europe? Where are corrections to radio information to be found?

Exercise 2

Navigational Lights and Buoyage

1 The diagrams below show the characteristics and periods of navigational lights. Describe and give the period of each light.

In addition, give the abbreviations that would be used, first in the older form and then in the new international system.

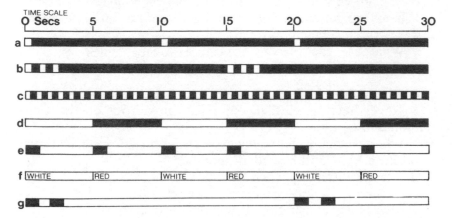

2 On which side should the following buoys be left when **leaving** harbour?

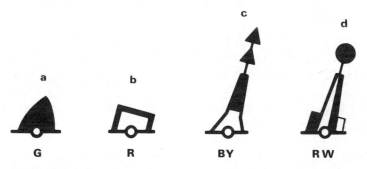

3 Draw a diagram to illustrate the colour, topmark and shape of each of the following buoys:

a Isolated danger
b East cardinal
c South cardinal
d West cardinal

4 On which side should buoys with the following characteristics be left when entering harbour?

a Flashing green
b Very Quick Flashing (6) + Long Flash

c Very Quick Flashing (9)
d Flashing red

5 What are the limitations of buoys as navigational aids which makes total reliance on them inadvisable?

6 A light is described in the light list as 'White 030°–180° (150°), Red 180°–205° (25°)'. Draw a diagram to show the sectors over which the red and white lights are visible.

7 The description of the Tongue Light Vessel includes the figures and letters '12m 24M'. What do they mean?

8 What sound is emitted from the following types of fog signal?
a Diaphone
b Nautophone
c Typhon
d Whistle

Exercise 3

Magnetic Compass – Variation and Deviation

Use the specimen deviation table provided in the data section.

1 What magnetic course should be steered to achieve a true course of 125° if the variation is 9° west?

2 A yacht is steering a course of 240°(M). Variation is 6° east. What is her true course?

3 The following magnetic bearings are taken to fix a yacht's position:

Lighthouse   022°(M)
Church   066°(M)
Windmill   138°(M)

Variation is 12° west. What should be the true bearings plotted?

4 What compass course should be steered to achieve a true course of 310° if the variation is 4° east?

5 A yacht is steering a course of 170°(C). Variation is 7° east. What is her true course?

6 A yacht is steering a course of 125°(C) when the following bearings are taken to fix her position:

Chimney   207°(C)
Beacon   245°(C)
Lighthouse   303°(C)

Variation is 8° west. What is her true course and what should be the true bearings plotted?

7 In 1984 you are navigating using a chart on which the variation is shown on the nearest compass rose as '9°10'W (1978) decreasing 8' annually'. What variation should you apply to magnetic bearings to convert them to true bearings?

8 You are sailing in a yacht in which the deviation of the compass is not known (do not use the specimen deviation table). The course is 260°(C) when the following bearings are taken to fix her position:

Headland ∅ Lighthouse   342°(C)
Church   019°(C)
Flagstaff   061°(C)

The chart shows that the bearing of the headland in transit with the lighthouse is 339°(T). Variation is 8° west. What is the yacht's true course and what would be the true bearings plotted?

9 You have taken delivery of a new yacht and are swinging the compass for deviation using the distant object method. The distant object is six miles away and you have calculated that from the position in which you are swinging the compass it should bear 228°(M). How close to the predetermined position must you remain in order to ensure that the bearing of the distant object is never inaccurate by more than ½°?

During the swing the following compass bearings of the distant object are taken.

Ship's head (Compass)	Compass bearing of distant object	Ship's head (Compass)	Compass bearing of distant object
000°	226°	180°	232°
022½°	224½°	202½°	233°
045°	223°	225°	234½°
067½°	223°	247½°	233½°
090°	225°	270°	232°
112½°	226½°	292½°	230°
135°	228°	315°	228½°
157½°	230°	337½°	227½°

Make out a deviation table for the compass.

10 A yacht is steering a course of 040°(C). The navigator standing in the companionway finds that with the hand bearing compass the apparent heading is 043°(C). The deviation of the steering compass is known to be as shown on the specimen deviation table. What is the deviation of the hand bearing compass? Would you expect the deviation of this compass to be the same if it was used at the after end of the cockpit?

Part II
Basic Chartwork

Exercise 4 consists of questions on working out position from course steered, distance run, tidal stream and leeway. The process involved is simple and logical: you plot the direction and distance the yacht has travelled under her own power, remembering that if she is making any leeway she does not move in the direction she is pointing, and then add any movement of the water in which she is floating, the tidal stream.

Exercise 5 tests ability to work out a course to steer to counteract tidal stream and leeway. This is a subject with which many Yachtmaster candidates have difficulty. Working out a course to steer to counteract tidal stream involves drawing a triangle of velocities and this can conveniently be done on the chart. Difficulties arise because distances are also plotted on the chart and clear thinking is required to avoid confusing distances and velocities. In all but the simplest problems it is necessary to make approximations, and there is an understandable reluctance to do this; until you are used to the method it seems to be a form of cheating. The questions in this exercise start simply, with the various complications being introduced one at a time.

Exercise 6 illustrates the various types of position fix. It does not deal with the special types of fix such as doubling the angle on the bow and the four-point bearing, as these are merely special cases of the basic running fix and the provisions which have to be met in order to use them seem unnecessary complications. Two crucial parts of fixing, selecting the method and taking bearings, cannot be tested without going to sea. The questions asked do, however, give an indication of the methods which are appropriate in certain circumstances and the order of inaccuracies which are likely to arise in practice.

Exercise 4

Dead Reckoning and Estimated Position

Use the specimen deviation table in the Data Section (page 35) and variation 6°W.

1 At 1430 a yacht takes departure from Broadstairs Knoll buoy, log reading 1.7, course 045°(C). The wind is from the north and she is making an estimated 10° leeway. The tidal stream is slack. At 1530 the log reading is 6.1. Plot the yacht's position at 1530.

2 At 1700 a yacht takes departure from position 180°(T) Outer Tongue buoy 1M, log reading 18.4, course 255°(C). The tidal stream is setting 330°(T) 3 knots and the yacht is making no leeway. At 1745 the log reading is 21.5. Plot the yacht's position at 1745. What has been her course and speed made good between 1700 and 1745?

3 At 1100 a yacht takes departure from position 000°(T) Margate Sand beacon 0.5M, log reading 18.4, course 245°(M). The wind is from the south, she is making 10° leeway and the tidal stream is setting 040°(T) 1.2 knots. At 1215 the log reading is 88.0. Plot the yacht's position at 1215. What has been her course and speed made good between 1100 and 1215?

4 At 0830 a yacht is at Spaniard buoy, log reading 11.7, steering 070°(M) closehauled on starboard tack, making 5° leeway. At 0855, log reading 14.0, she tacks onto port, steering 165°(M) and continuing to make 5° leeway. At 0930 the log reading is 16.6. The tidal stream between 0830 and 0930 is setting 110°(T) 1.4 knots. Plot the yacht's position at 0930.

5 At 1100 a yacht takes departure from Medway No.4 buoy, log reading 2.9, steering 120°(M), leeway negligible. At 1150, log reading 5.8, she is at the Spile buoy. What has been the direction and rate of the tidal stream between 1100 and 1150?

6 The extract of the log below is for a yacht on passage eastward from Ramsgate:

Time	Log	Co.(M)	Leeway	Remarks
0640	31.3	120°	5°	Position 090°(T) N Goodwin Lt V 1.0M. Closehauled on port tack.
0700	32.8	120°	5°	
0715	34.0			Tacked onto starboard, steering 020°(M).
0800	36.8	020°	5°	Wind headed. Altered course 005°(M).
0900	39.1	005°	5°	

Tidal stream predictions are:

0600–0700: 080°(T) 2.4 knots
0700–0800: 110°(T) 2.0 knots
0800–0900: 190°(T) 1.1 knots

Plot the yacht's position at 0900.

Exercise 5

Course to Steer to Counteract Tidal Stream and Leeway

Note For the purposes of this exercise it is assumed that there is no shipping in the Thames Estuary. The questions are about shaping course between two points and do not concern the advisability of crossing a shipping lane at an oblique angle.

1 What is the course to steer to make good a course of 240°(T) if the tidal stream is setting 170°(T) 1.7 knots and the yacht's speed is 5 knots? What will be the speed make good?

2   At 0900 a yacht is at Swin Spitway buoy, making 3 knots through the water. Leeway is negligible. If the tidal stream is setting 075°(T) 1.5 knots, what is her course to steer to N Hook Middle buoy and at what time will she arrive there?

3   On a long cross-tide leg which will take several hours to sail, is it better to alter course each hour as the rate of the stream changes in order to stay on the direct line or to steer one course which allows for the stream throughout the passage, allowing the yacht to follow a curving track to her destination?

4   A yacht is in position 000°(T) Tongue Light Vessel 0.5M at 1400, heading through Fisherman's Gat towards Black Deep No. 8 Buoy at 3.5 knots. Leeway is negligible. It is just before high water and the tidal streams for the next three hours are:
1400–1500: 260°(T) 0.8 knots
1500–1600: 250°(T) 1.9 knots
1600–1700: 254°(T) 2.1 knots
What is her course to steer?

5   A yacht is at Wallet Spitway Buoy heading towards Colne Bar buoy at 4 knots. The wind is from the southwest and she is making 10° leeway. If the tidal stream is setting 070°(T) 1.9 knots, what is her course to steer?

6   At 1700 a yacht is at East Tongue buoy heading through Princes Channel towards Girdler buoy at 3.5 knots. The wind is from the north and she is making 5° leeway. The tidal streams for the next four hours are:
1700–1800: 070°(T) 1.8 knots
1800–1900: 060°(T) 1.1 knots
1900–2000: 060°(T) 0.2 knots
2000–2100: 290°(T) 0.6 knots

What is her course to steer and at what time will she reach Girdler buoy? Plot the position of the yacht at 1800 and 1900.

7   At 1500 a yacht is at SE Mouse buoy steering 250°(T) at 4.5 knots, closehauled on the starboard tack, making 5° leeway. The tidal stream is setting 080° (T) 1.5 knots. At what time should she tack to lay the SW Swin buoy and what should be the bearing of the buoy when she tacks? Assume that the yacht turns through 95° between tacks.

Exercise 6

Position Fixing

Use variation 6° W.

1   A yacht is approaching the south of the Thames Estuary by night and the following bearings are taken:

0315	Tongue Light Vessel	309°(M)
	N Foreland Light	244°(M)
	N Goodwin Light Vessel	191°(M)

Plot the yacht's position at 0315.

2   What criteria would you apply to the selection of the marks for a three-bearing visual fix?

3   Comment on the suitability of the following as fixing marks:
a   An edge of land
b   A flagstaff
c   A buoy
d   The summit of a hill
e   A conspicuous block of flats
f   The point at which a railway line enters a tunnel

4   The intersection of two position lines will give a position, so why is it considered good navigational practice to use three bearings for a visual fix?

5   How far will a position line resulting from a visual bearing be displaced from its true position if the mark used is 6 sea miles away and the bearing is 3° in error?

6 a yacht is approaching the southern part of the Thames Estuary in moderate visibility, steering 250°(M). She is making no leeway and the tidal stream is slack.
At 1420, log reading 26.4, S Knock buoy bears 332°(M).
At 1455, log reading 28.9, S Knock buoy bears 018°(M).
Plot the yacht's position at 1455.

7 A yacht is on passage to seaward out of Fisherman's Gat, steering 140°(M) and making no leeway. The tidal stream is setting 080°(T) at 2.4 knots.
At 2315, log reading 12.4, Tongue Light Vessel bears 206°(M).
At 2345, log reading 15.1, Tongue Light Vessel bears 262°(M).
Plot the yacht's position at 2345.

8 A yacht is entering Margate Roads from the northeast in poor visibility, steering 240°(M) and making no leeway.
At 1300, log reading 35.7, NE Spit buoy bears 023°(M).
At 1312, log reading 36.8, E Margate buoy bears 346°(M).
The tidal stream is setting 280°(T) at 3 knots.
Plot the yacht's position at 1312.

9 A yacht is approaching Kentish Knock from the northeast. At 0128 the depth, reduced to datum, is 10 metres, shoaling, the Kentish Knock buoy bears 084°(M). Plot her position at 0128.

10 A yacht is on passage through the Barrow Swatchway, steering with Barrow No. 9 buoy in transit with SW Sunk beacon, bearing 089°(M). At 0823 the Barrow beacon is in transit with Whittaker beacon, bearing 341°(M). Plot the yacht's position at 0823 and comment on the reliability of the fix.

Part III
Tides

The prediction of tidal heights is a subject which is complicated by the existence of a number of different forms of tide table and several different methods of working.

The most comprehensive and accurate table in general use is the Admiralty Tide Table. It also has the advantage of presenting information in a highly visual form, with curves representing the rise and fall of tide between high and low water. Its disadvantages, for use in a yacht, are that it is bulky and relatively expensive.

The majority of yachtsmen tend to use the tide tables in *Reed's Nautical Almanac*. These tables are inherently less accurate than the ATT but they exist as part of a book which provides a complete set of nautical tables and they are therefore extremely convenient to use. An extract from the *Reed's* tide table is reprinted in the Data section of this book, to provide predictions for one month for ports in the Thames Estuary. A table for calculating rise and fall of tide is also given. This is the simpler of two such tables in the *Almanac*; it is the less accurate but it is the easier of the two to use.

Exercise 7

Tidal Calculations

All times given in this exercise are BST (GMT + 1). Answers should also be expressed in BST.

1 What is the least height of tide which will allow a yacht drawing 1.8m to cross a shoal of charted depth 0.6m with a clearance of 0.5m?

2 A yacht which draws 1.5m is lying dried out against a harbour wall. The depth in the berth is charted as drying 1.2m. What will be the height of tide when the yacht re-floats?

3 What is the height of North Foreland light above sea level when the height of tide at Margate is 2.1m?

4 What will be the time and height of low water in the middle of the day at Harwich on Thursday 27 August?

5 At what time on the morning of Sunday 9 August will the tide reach a height of 2.5m at Sheerness?

6 At what time during the afternoon of Saturday 8 August will the tide reach a height of 3.8m at Burnham-on-Crouch?

7 What will be the height of tide at Dover at 1400 on Friday 7 August?

8 What will be the height of tide at Harwich at 2100 on Monday 24 August?

9 What will be the times and heights of the high and low waters before noon at Ramsgate on Friday 21 August?

10 What will be the times and heights of high water and low water at Orford Haven Bar after noon on Monday 10 August?

11 What effect would you expect a low barometer and prolonged easterly gales to have on tidal times and heights in the Thames Estuary?

12 What are the relative merits of the following three sources of tidal stream information?
a Tidal stream atlas
b Tidal diamonds on a chart
c Tidal stream notes in sailing directions

27

Part IV
Navigation in Practice

Exercise 8 deals with pilotage. In this context pilotage is considered as navigation by eye, with reference to the chart and compass but without actually plotting on the chart. It is used in confined waters where the scale of the chart and the frequency of course alterations make plotting on the chart unrealistic.

Exercises 9 poses passage planning problems. This is a large subject, involving the selection of sailing times, deciding the most advantageous courses and generally pre-working the passage to avoid unnecessary problems. By skilful planning it is possible to reduce the amount of work that has to be done at sea. However it is possible to over-plan, with a consequent loss of flexibility.

Exercise 10, as far as possible, poses problems in the way they are likely to occur at sea so it is more than just an exercise in navigational techniques. Carrying out navigational techniques is relatively easy, given the necessary factual information on which to base them. The art, as opposed to the science, of navigation lies in deciding which facts can be gathered and how reliable they are likely to be. This art can only be developed fully at sea but the final exercise provides a number of pointers to the skills which have to be developed and the pitfalls to be avoided.

Exercise 8
Pilotage

1   One facet of pilotage is the selection of an anchor berth. What are the general criteria which would influence your

choice of an anchor berth for a 24 hour stay? Give the reasons why you would seek certain features and avoid others.

2   You are on passage from Margate bound towards the Swale in a yacht which draws 1.5m. Visibility is good, the wind is SW 5 close under the land but stronger to seaward. It is just before low water (height of tide 2m) and you have been hugging the shore to stay in calm water and keep out of the full force of the ebb stream. You are short-handed and you would prefer not to have to take fixes.

In the final stages of the passage how would you ensure that you cleared the end of Whitstable Street and Whitstable flats without having to go any further to seaward than necessary and without having to take frequent fixes?

3   You are on passage from the Blackwater towards Harwich in a yacht drawing 1.5m. The wind is northeasterly and it is half flood (height of tide 2m). After passing Clacton you decide to short-tack along the shore to keep out of the full force of the adverse stream. How will you make sure that you do not run aground on the inshore legs of the beat between Clacton and Walton Pier?

4   You are on passage from the Crouch towards the Medway. The wind is SW and the tidal stream ebbing. After rounding S Whitaker buoy would it be safe to rely on the echosounder to give a clearing line on which to go about at the end of each port tack? Give reasons for your answer.

5   A yacht is on passage, motoring from the Swale by way of the West Swin towards the Crouch on a wet and windless night. The tidal stream is flooding strongly. Shortly after passing to the west of North Red Sand buoy the skipper sights the SW Barrow buoy, Qk Fl(6) + LFl, and tells the helmsman to steer for it. The skipper then retires below to the chart table.

The next mark is the SW Swin buoy, which the skipper says is Gp Fl(2) Red and the helmsman sights it right ahead just before reaching SW Barrow.

29

Approaching SW Swin the skipper asks the helmsman to look out for Maplin buoy, Qk Fl(3), and the helmsman reports that he sees it, again right ahead.

The next mark is Maplin Bank buoy and the skipper gives its characteristic as Gp Fl(3) Red. this time the helmsman says that he sees a red flasher ahead but the characteristic seems wrong. The skipper comes on deck and finds that the buoy ahead is Fl Red 2.5 seconds and there seem to be too many other lights around. What has gone wrong and why has it gone wrong?

6 Many small creeks are marked by withies. What are withies and what particular characteristics are you likely to find in creeks and channels marked by them?

7 Many river entrances have bars which dry or carry very little depth at low water. Entry to these rivers may, under certain circumstances, be extremely hazardous even though there is very little risk of grounding on the bar. Why is this?

8 Piloting a yacht in a narrow channel, some skippers like to take the helm themselves. Others prefer one of the crew to steer. What are the relative advantages of each method and what skills are necessary to overcome the potential difficulties inherent in each of them?

9 You are about to enter an estuary in which the channel between mud flats is narrow and tortuous but well marked. You have visited it before but you do not know it well. Your engine has been unreliable recently so you decide to make the entry under sail. Out at sea there is a steady force 3 and the land around the estuary is low-lying so there should be a similar breeze inside. You are approaching the estuary sailing fast under full main and large genoa, with the yacht well secured for sea. What preparations should you make to the yacht before you reach the entrance to the channel?

Exercise 9

Passage Planning

1 Explain how the following factors are likely to affect a passage plan.

a   Tidal heights
b   Tidal streams
c   Time of day
d   Hours of daylight/darkness
e   Forecast wind direction and strength
f   Ranges of navigational lights
g   Phase of the moon
h   Traffic separation schemes

2 On a passage round North Foreland towards the River Crouch there are a number of possible routes. Assuming that the passage is being made in daylight, that there is sufficient rise of tide and that arrival at the Crouch is timed for high water, what are the relative merits and drawbacks of the three routes described below?

a   Through North Edinburgh Channel, to SW Sunk beacon and north of East Barrow Sand.
b   Through South Edinburgh Channel, across Tizard Bank, north of Knock John Nos. 1 and 2 buoys to the Mid Barrow, through Barrow Swatchway to Barrow Beacon and round the east end of Foulness Sand.
c   Through Fisherman's Gat, across Black Deep to the Sunk Beacon, and north of Middle Sunk and East Barrow sands.

3 You are on passage from the Solent towards Sheerness. You hoped to be round North Foreland during the late forenoon on 4 August to carry the tide up the Gore, Horse and Four Fathoms Channels. Light winds during the early part of the passage have delayed you and you do not round the Longnose buoy until 0030 on 5 August. The wind is now SSW 4

31

and you are making 4½ knots on a close reach. First light is at 0430. Visibility is 5 miles.

Explain why you would prefer either to continue along the route you had previously planned, stand out to the north and make the passage through the Queens Channel, or anchor off Margate and wait for daylight.

4   You are the skipper of a 7.5m bilge-keeler. She draws 1.1m and the sailing performance you expect from her is:

	Force 4		Force 6	
	speed	leeway	speed	leeway
Beating	3½ knots	10°	2½ knots	20°
Reaching	5½ knots	5°	4½ knots	10°
Running	5 knots	–	5½ knots	–

Under power she makes 5 knots in calm water and 2½ knots into a force 6 in the open sea.

On the evening of Wednesday 5 August you are at anchor in the River Deben. You have arranged to pick up another crew member in the East Swale late on the evening of Thursday 6 August. You have been delayed by strong winds; it has been blowing hard from the SW all afternoon and the 1750 forecast for sea area Thames was SW 6–8, veering NW 4–6, rain then showers, moderate becoming good.

What will be your general tactics for the passage to the Swale, including time of sailing from the Deben, route across the Thames Estuary, time at which you hope to arrive at the Swale, and the factors which influence your decisions on the passage plan?

Exercise 10

Passage Making

Use variation 6° W.

1 You are the skipper of a yacht making for the River Blackwater from the east in visibility of about ¾ mile. At 0900 on 30 August you are in estimated position 51° 54′ N, 1° 45′ E; it is calm and you are motoring at 4 knots. It is 12 hours since your last reliable fix. How will you make your landfall?

2 Continuing from question 1. At 0905 you obtain a faint signal from radio beacon callsign UK on 312.6 kHz. The null extends to about 40°, giving an approximate bearing of either 245°(M) or 065°(M). The depth by echosounder is 24m. What course should you now steer? Give reasons for your answer.

3 Continuing from question 2. At 0948 the signal from beacon callsign UK is considerably stronger and it bears 242°(M). At 0949 a beacon transmitting on 305.7 kHz is picked up, bearing 211°(M). The callsign of this beacon is unreadable but the transmission commences at 0949 precisely. At 0950 a beacon callsign NF transmitting on 301.1 kHz bears 204°(M). The depth by echosounder is still 24m. What are the three radio beacons? Plot the three bearings obtained and comment on the results.

4 Continuing from question 3. At 1100 the yacht is at Sunk Light Vessel and the visibility is improving. As it will not be possible to make the Blackwater on this tide you decide to head for Walton Backwaters. What is the course to steer to leave South Cork buoy 0.5 mile to starboard?

5 Continuing from question 4. At 1100 you take departure from Sunk Light Vessel, log reading 91.4, steering 310°(M), speed 4 knots. Plot the yacht's position at 1130.

At 1130 the log reads 93.4 and the following bearings are taken:

1130	Roughs Tower	338°(M)
	South Shipwash buoy	068°(M)
	Sunk Light Vessel	109°(M)

Assuming that the log and course have been correct, what has been the direction and rate of the tidal stream between 1100 and 1130?

6 You are the skipper of a yacht on passage from the Swale bound towards Harwich on 16 August. Visibility is about 0.5M, the wind is NE 3 and you can lay 010°(T) on starboard, 100°(T) on port tack, at 4 knots. Leeway is negligible. At 1445 you are at Heaps buoy, log reading 10.0, making for Gunfleet Spit buoy. Describe in detail how you will make this leg of the passage.

Part V
Data Section

Specimen Deviation Table

Ship's head (Compass)	Deviation	Ship's head (Compass)	Deviation
000°	7°E	180°	7°W
022½°	4°E	202½°	6°W
045°	2°E	225°	5°W
067½°	0	247½°	2°W
090°	1°W	270°	1°E
112½°	3°W	292½°	3°E
135°	6°W	315°	5°E
157½°	7°W	337½°	8°E

RISE AND FALL OF TIDE TABLE

h min.	0.5	1.0	1.5	2.0	2.5	3.0	3.5	4.0	4.5	5.0	5.5	6.0	6.5	7.0	7.5	8.0	8.5	9.0	9.5	10.0
										RANGE OF THE TIDE IN METRES										
0 20	0.0	0.0	0.0	0.0	0.0	0.0	0.0	0.0	0.0	0.0	0.0	0.0	0.1	0.1	0.1	0.1	0.1	0.1	0.1	0.1
40	0.0	0.0	0.0	0.1	0.1	0.1	0.1	0.1	0.1	0.2	0.2	0.2	0.2	0.2	0.2	0.2	0.3	0.3	0.3	0.3
1 00	0.0	0.1	0.1	0.1	0.2	0.2	0.2	0.3	0.3	0.3	0.4	0.4	0.4	0.5	0.5	0.5	0.6	0.6	0.6	0.7
20	0.1	0.1	0.2	0.2	0.3	0.4	0.4	0.5	0.5	0.6	0.6	0.7	0.8	0.8	0.9	0.9	1.0	1.1	1.1	1.2
40	0.1	0.2	0.3	0.4	0.4	0.5	0.6	0.7	0.8	0.9	1.0	1.1	1.2	1.2	1.3	1.4	1.5	1.6	1.7	1.8
2 00	0.1	0.3	0.4	0.5	0.6	0.8	0.9	1.0	1.1	1.3	1.4	1.5	1.6	1.8	1.9	2.0	2.1	2.3	2.4	2.5
20	0.2	0.3	0.5	0.7	0.8	1.0	1.1	1.3	1.5	1.6	1.8	2.0	2.1	2.3	2.5	2.6	2.8	3.0	3.1	3.3
40	0.2	0.4	0.6	0.8	1.0	1.2	1.4	1.7	1.9	2.1	2.3	2.5	2.7	2.9	3.1	3.3	3.5	3.7	3.9	4.1
3 00	0.3	0.5	0.8	1.0	1.3	1.5	1.8	2.0	2.3	2.5	2.8	3.0	3.3	3.5	3.8	4.0	4.3	4.5	4.8	5.0
20	0.3	0.6	0.9	1.2	1.5	1.8	2.1	2.3	2.6	2.9	3.2	3.5	3.8	4.1	4.4	4.7	5.0	5.3	5.6	5.9
40	0.3	0.7	1.0	1.3	1.7	2.0	2.4	2.7	3.0	3.4	3.7	4.0	4.4	4.7	5.0	5.4	5.7	6.0	6.4	6.7
4 00	0.4	0.8	1.1	1.5	1.9	2.3	2.6	3.0	3.4	3.8	4.1	4.5	4.9	5.3	5.6	6.0	6.4	6.8	7.1	7.5
20	0.4	0.8	1.2	1.6	2.1	2.5	2.9	3.3	3.7	4.1	4.5	4.9	5.3	5.8	6.2	6.6	7.0	7.4	7.8	8.2
40	0.4	0.9	1.3	1.8	2.2	2.6	3.1	3.5	4.0	4.4	4.9	5.3	5.7	6.2	6.6	7.1	7.5	7.9	8.4	8.9
5 00	0.5	0.9	1.4	1.9	2.3	2.8	3.3	3.7	4.2	4.7	5.1	5.6	6.1	6.5	7.0	7.5	7.9	8.4	8.9	9.3
20	0.5	1.0	1.5	1.9	2.4	2.9	3.4	3.9	4.4	4.9	5.3	5.8	6.3	6.8	7.3	7.8	8.2	8.7	9.2	9.7
40	0.5	1.0	1.5	2.0	2.5	3.0	3.5	4.0	4.5	5.0	5.5	6.0	6.4	6.9	7.4	7.9	8.4	8.9	9.4	9.9
6 00	0.5	1.0	1.5	2.0	2.5	3.0	3.5	4.0	4.5	5.0	5.5	6.0	6.5	7.0	7.5	8.0	8.5	9.0	9.5	10.0

EXAMPLE. Find the Range of the Tide first. The range of a tide is the difference in height between the level of any high water and that of the preceding or succeeding low water. If H.W. is 5.5m. and following L.W. is 0.7m. then the Range of that particular tide is 4.8m. How much will this tide fall below H.W. in 2h. 20min.? The table shows (by interpolation) that this fall is 1.6m.

TIDAL DIFFERENCES ON DOVER

PLACE	MHW		ML	DMR	RULING DEPTH AT			
	Tm. Diff. h. min.	Ht. Diff. m.	m.	h. min	HWS m.	HWN m.	CD m.	POSITION
Hastings	−0 05	+0.6	4.0	5 30	9.0	7.3	1.5	Entrance
Rye (Apprs.)	0 00	+0.8	—	—	6.2	4.5	−1.5	Bar near entrance
Dungeness	−0 15	+1.2	4.4	5 00	15.3	13.6	7.3	West Road Anche.
Folkestone	−0 10	+0.4	3.9	5 00	5.5	3.1	−1.6	Alongside Sth. Quay
Dover	0 00	0.0	3.7	5 05	7.1	5.7	0.4	Entce. Granville Dock
Deal	+0.15	−0.4	3.5	5 10	10.1	9.0	4.0	Pier Head
Richborough	+0 15	−1.0	3.0	5 20	2.8	1.7	−0.9	Chan. to
Ramsgate	+0 20	−1.6	2.6	5 30	5.0	3.9	0.1	Entrance

DOVER

G.M.T.

SHEERNESS

DOVER — AUGUST

	Time h.min.	Ht. m.		Time h.min.	Ht. m.
1 Sa	0713	0.9	**16** Su	0638	1.0
	1144	6.7		1118	6.6
	1927	0.8		1902	0.9
	—	—		2332	6.5
2 Su	0004	6.6	**17** M	0717	0.9
	0759	0.9		1156	6.7
	1224	6.7		1938	0.8
	2011	0.7		—	—
3 M	0043	6.5	**18** Tu	0011	6.6
	0837	0.9		0749	0.9
	1302	6.7		1236	6.8
	2050	0.8		2009	0.8
4 Tu	0123	6.4	**19** W	0055	6.6
	0910	1.1		0819	0.9
	1340	6.6		1317	6.7
	2124	1.0		2042	0.8
5 W	0201	6.2	**20** Th	0138	6.5
	0936	1.4		0854	0.9
	1419	6.4		1359	6.6
	2155	1.3		2119	0.9
6 Th	0243	6.0	**21** F	0226	6.3
	1000	1.6		0934	1.1
	1501	6.2		1446	6.3
	2226	1.5		2200	1.1
7 F	0328	5.7	**22** Sa	0317	6.1
	1031	1.9		1020	1.4
	1549	5.9		1538	6.1
	2302	1.8		2251	1.4
8 Sa	0421	5.4	**23**	0416	5.8
	1112	2.1		1115	1.7
	1645	5.5		1641	5.8
	2349	2.1		2357	1.7
9 Su	0529	5.2	**24** M	0525	5.6
	1205	2.4		1229	1.9
	1757	5.3		1756	5.6
	—	—		—	—
10 M	0046	2.2	**25** Tu	0120	1.9
	0650	5.1		0648	5.5
	1313	2.4		1357	1.9
	1917	5.2		1923	5.6
11 Tu	0158	2.2	**26** W	0249	1.7
	0801	5.3		0816	5.7
	1437	2.3		1521	1.6
	2020	5.4		2047	5.8
12 W	0317	2.0	**27** Th	0406	1.5
	0853	5.6		0922	6.0
	1550	1.9		1633	1.3
	2110	5.6		2148	6.1
13 Th	0416	1.7	**28** F	0515	1.2
	0934	5.9		1009	6.3
	1644	1.5		1734	1.0
	2148	5.9		2233	6.4
14 F	0506	1.3	**29** Sa	0614	1.0
	1009	6.2		1048	6.6
	1733	1.2		1829	0.8
	2220	6.1		2309	6.5
15 Sa	0554	1.1	**30** Su	0702	0.9
	1042	6.4		1125	6.7
	1818	1.0		1914	0.8
	2254	6.4		2344	6.5
			31 M	0741	0.9
				1201	6.8
				1952	0.8

SHEERNESS — AUGUST

	Time h.min.	Ht. m.		Time h.min.	Ht. m.
1 Sa	0103	5.9	**16** Su	0049	5.7
	0723	0.7		0652	0.7
	1324	5.8		1306	5.7
	1954	0.3		1924	0.6
2 Su	0148	6.0	**17** M	0130	5.9
	0805	0.7		0737	0.7
	1408	5.9		1345	5.8
	2037	0.3		2011	0.5
3 M	0232	6.0	**18** Tu	0209	5.9
	0843	0.8		0819	0.7
	1449	5.8		1423	5.9
	2118	0.5		2054	0.5
4 Tu	0312	5.9	**19** W	0250	5.9
	0919	0.9		0900	0.8
	1527	5.7		1501	5.9
	2153	0.7		2135	0.6
5 W	0352	5.7	**20** Th	0331	5.8
	0949	1.1		0935	0.9
	1603	5.5		1541	5.8
	2223	0.9		2210	0.7
6 Th	0428	5.4	**21** F	0413	5.6
	1016	1.3		1007	1.0
	1640	5.3		1621	5.7
	2249	1.1		2242	0.9
7 F	0506	5.2	**22** Sa	0458	5.4
	1047	1.4		1045	1.2
	1720	5.1		1708	5.5
	2323	1.2		2320	1.1
8 Sa	0550	5.0	**23** Su	0551	5.1
	1127	1.5		1134	1.3
	1808	4.9		1807	5.2
9 Su	0012	1.4	**24** M	0017	1.3
	0641	4.7		0657	4.9
	1227	1.7		1245	1.4
	1909	4.6		1923	5.0
10 M	0120	1.5	**25** Tu	0137	1.4
	0745	4.6		0815	4.9
	1347	1.8		1416	1.4
	2022	4.5		2047	5.1
11 Tu	0237	1.5	**26** W	0311	1.4
	0857	4.6		0931	5.1
	1510	1.6		1552	1.2
	2139	4.6		2206	5.3
12 W	0341	1.3	**27** Th	0431	1.2
	1004	4.8		1040	5.4
	1612	1.4		1709	0.8
	2240	4.9		2311	5.6
13 Th	0433	1.1	**28** F	0533	1.0
	1058	5.1		1137	5.6
	1702	1.1		1807	0.6
	2327	5.2		—	—
14 F	0520	1.0	**29** Sa	0004	5.8
	1143	5.4		0622	0.8
	1750	0.9		1225	5.7
				1855	0.4
15 Sa	0010	5.5	**30** Su	0050	5.9
	0605	0.8		0704	0.8
	1225	5.6		1307	5.8
	1838	0.8		1937	0.4
			31 M	0131	5.9
				0742	0.7
				1347	5.8
				2015	0.4

HARWICH

BURNHAM -ON- CROUCH

HIGH WATER G.M.T.

D of W	AUGUST Time h. min.	Ht. m.	Time h. min.	Ht. m.	Day of Month	D of W	AUGUST Time h. min.	Ht. m.	Time h. min.	Ht. m.
Sa	0012	4.0	1236	4.0	1	Sa	0054	5.5	1314	5.4
Su	0058	4.1	1320	4.0	2	Su	0138	5.6	1356	5.5
M	0143	4.1	1403	4.0	3	M	0221	5.6	1435	5.5
Tu	0226	4.0	1443	3.9	4	Tu	0259	5.5	1512	5.4
W	0306	3.9	1521	3.8	5	W	0337	5.3	1549	5.3
Th	0346	3.7	1557	3.7	6	Th	0414	5.1	1626	5.1
F	0424	3.5	1634	3.5	7	F	0454	4.9	1707	4.8
Sa	0504	3.3	1716	3.4	8	Sa	0538	4.7	1759	4.6
Su	0553	3.2	1810	3.3	9	Su	0634	4.5	1902	4.4
M	0659	3.2	1932	3.2	10	M	0739	4.4	2019	4.3
Tu	0816	3.3	2048	3.4	11	Tu	0856	4.4	2139	4.4
W	0918	3.5	2144	3.5	12	W	1000	4.6	2295	4.6
Th	1009	3.7	2231	3.7	13	Th	1052	4.9	2319	4.9
F	1055	3.9	2313	3.9	14	F	1136	5.1	—	—
Sa	1137	4.0	2355	4.0	15	Sa	0002	5.2	1218	5.3
Su	—	—	1217	4.0	16	Su	0043	5.4	1259	5.5
M	0036	4.1	1257	4.0	17	M	0123	5.6	1338	5.6
Tu	0118	4.1	1338	4.0	18	Tu	0201	5.7	1414	5.7
W	0201	4.1	1418	4.1	19	W	0240	5.7	1451	5.7
Th	0244	4.0	1456	4.0	20	Th	0319	5.6	1528	5.6
F	0326	3.9	1536	4.0	21	F	0400	5.4	1607	5.5
Sa	0410	3.7	1619	3.8	22	Sa	0445	5.2	1654	5.3
Su	0459	3.4	1714	3.6	23	Su	0538	4.9	1755	5.1
M	0606	3.3	1831	3.5	24	M	0647	4.8	1914	4.9
Tu	0727	3.3	1958	3.5	25	Tu	0807	4.8	2042	4.9
W	0842	3.4	2112	3.7	26	W	0928	4.9	2203	5.0
Th	0947	3.6	2215	3.8	27	Th	1033	5.0	2305	5.2
F	1044	3.8	2310	4.0	28	F	1128	5.2	2357	5.4
Sa	1134	3.9	2358	4.1	29	Sa	—	—	1215	5.4
Su	—	—	1219	4.0	30	Su	0042	5.5	1257	5.5
M	0042	4.1	1300	4.0	31	M	0121	5.6	1335	5.5

Place	Mean H.W. Time Difference	Height Difference	Mean Level	Duration of Mean Rise	Ruling depth at H.W. Springs	H.W. Neaps	Chart Datum	Position
	h. min.	m.	m.	h. min.	m.	m.	m.	
Paglesham	+0 10	—	3.0	6 15	5.5	4.5	0.0	At end of slip
BURNHAM-ON-CROUCH	0 00	0.0	3.0	6 10	9.5	8.5	4.0	Bar off R.C Yacht Club
Fambridge	+0 10	-0.1	—	—	—	—	—	
Hullbridge	+0 15	-0.1	3.0	6 15	4.4	3.4	-1.1	At Quay
Battlesbridge	+0 25	—	—	—	—	—	—	
Buxey Beacon	-0 10	-0.5	2.8	6 15	3.8	2.9	-0.9	Ray Sand Chan Bar

TIDAL DIFFERENCES ON SHEERNESS

PLACE	MHW Tm. Diff. h. min.	MHW Ht. Diff. m.	ML m.	DMR h. min.	RULING DEPTH AT HWS m.	RULING DEPTH AT HWN m.	RULING DEPTH AT CD m.	POSITION
Margate	-0 40	-0.9	2.6	6 10	2.1	1.2	-2.7	In Harbour
Herne Bay	-0 20	-0.5	2.9	6 05	6.2	5.3	1.7	Pier head
Whitstable	-0 15	-0.3	3.0	6 05	4.2	3.3	-1.2	Entrance
Harty Ferry	0 00	0.0	3.0	6 10	9.0	8.1	3.4	Channel
Pan Sano Hole ...	-0 35	-0.7	3.1	6 10	9.9	9.1	4.9	South of Beacon
S. Shingles By.	-0 40	-0.8	3.1	6 10	20.3	19.5	15.5	Princes Channel
Gt. Nore	-0 10	0.0	3.1	6 10	20.7	19.8	15.0	Anchorage for seagoing vessels only
Sheerness	0 00	0.0	3.1	6 10	17.7	16.8	12.0	Cornwallis Pier

TIDAL DIFFERENCES ON HARWICH

PLACE	MHW Tm. Diff. h. min.	MHW Ht. Diff. m.	ML m.	DMR h. min.	RULING DEPTH AT HWS m.	RULING DEPTH AT HWN m.	RULING DEPTH AT CD m.	POSITION
Sales Point	+0 15	—	—	—	—	—	-3.3	Over St. Peter's Flats
Tollesbury (Mill Creek)	+0 20	—	2.4	6 10	—	—	Dries	
Bradwell Quay	+0 20	+1.0	2.8	6 20	6.1	5.0	0.8	Chan. behind Pewit Is.
Osea Island	+0 40	+1.1	2.8	6 35	5.4	4.4	0.1	Pier Head
Maldon	+0 50	-1.2	—	6 15	3.2	2.6	0.3	Chan. off The Hythe
West Mersea	+0 25	+0.9	2.8	6 25	—	—	Dries	Hard
Brightlingsea	+0 15	+0.7	2.5	6 15	5.6	4.4	0.6	Bar to Creek
Wivenhoe	+0 25	—	—	—	—	—	-0.3	
Colchester	+0 30	—	—	—	3.4	—		Hythe Quay
Colne Point	0 10	+0.3	—	6 15	4.7	4.0	0.3	Colne bar
Walton-on-Naze ..	-0 10	+0.1	2.3	6 15	5.7	4.9	1.5	Bar
Hamford Water ...	-0 10	+0.1	2.3	6 20	4.7	4.1	0.6	Halliday Rock Flats
Harwich	0 00	0.0	2.2	6 30	9.5	8.9	5.5	Outer Pier
Parkstone Quay	0 00	0.0	2.2	6 30	9.5	8.9	5.5	Alongside Quay
Wrabness Point	+0 10	+0.1	2.2	6 00	6.8	6.1	2.7	Fairway by red buoy
Mistley Quay	+0 25	+0.1	2.2	5 45	4.2	3.4	0.0	Alongside quay
Manningtree	+0 30	+0.2	2.3	5 40	3.5	2.5	-1.0	At Quay
River Orwell								
Pinmill	+0 05	+0.1	2.2	5 50	10.0	9.2	5.8	Dredged channel
Downham Reach	+0 10	+0.1	2.2	5 50	10.0	9.2	5.8	Dredged channel
Ipswich	+0 20	+0.1	2.2	5 55	10.0	9.2	5.8	Dredged channel
Felixstowe	-0 15	-0.3	2.1	6 30	10.9	10.2	7.2	Channel to
Woodbridge	+0 45	-0.2	2.1	6 45	4.2	3.1	0.0	Chan
Deben River Bar	-0.15	-0.4	2.0	6 35	3.7	2.9	0.0	On Bar
Cork Lt. V.	-0 10	-0.5	1.8	6 25	—	—	6.8	Cork Anchorage
Orford Hn. Bar	-0 25	-0.8	1.8	6 40	5.4	4.8	2.2	Bar
Orford Quay	+0 30	-1.4	—	5 55	4.6	4.1	2.0	In river
Slaughden	+1 15	-1.6	—	—	4.3	4.0	2.1	In river
Snape Bridge	+3 15	-2.0	—	—	2.8	2.1	0.7	Channel
Shipwash Lt. V.	-0 05	—	—	—	—	—	9.0	Shipway channel
Hollesley Bay	-0 30	-1.2	1.2	6 15	11.3	10.7	8.4	Anchorage W. of Bank

Part VI
Answers to Exercises

Exercise 1

1

a 51° 20′.3N, 1° 34′.3E
   or 114°(T) N Foreland Light, 5.2M
b 51° 30′.6N, 1° 23′.0E
   or 344°(T) N Foreland Light 8.5M
c 51° 26′.2N, 1° 04′.2E
   or 285°(T) N Foreland Light, 14.6M

2

a Seabed is shingle and broken shells.
b Charted depth 11.5m below chart datum.
c Charted drying height 2.1m above chart datum.
d A wreck, dangerous to surface navigation, which dries.
e A wreck, 2.4m below chart datum.
f A recommended anchorage.

3
a A church.
b Charted drying height 7ft above chart datum.
c A beacon.
d Charted depth 4fath 3ft below chart datum.
e,g A rock with a depth of 6ft or less below chart datum.
f A tower.
h A 10fath depth contour line.
j Seabed is rock.
k A flagstaff.
l A wreck, not considered dangerous to surface navigation, the
position of which is approximate.

4

a 10 sea miles.

40

b 9.85 sea miles.

c The chart is drawn on a Mercator projection. The latitude scale is therefore not uniform but increases towards the northern end of the chart. The latitude scale represents distance only at that latitude and on a small-scale chart there will be a considerable difference between the charted representation of distance at the north and south ends of the chart.

5

a Only the largest scale chart contains the full detail of hazards, aids to navigation and topography.

b It is possible that the edge of the lower chart will protrude and it will be possible to use its latitude scale, rather than the latitude scale of the chart in use, for measuring distances. If the two charts are of different scale this will result in errors in plotting and measuring distance. The danger is greatest when the charts are of slightly different scale; if there is a large difference common sense should reveal the error.

c To guard against gross error when transferring from one chart to another.

d So that chartwork can be clearly visible but easy to erase.

e If the chart is wet the printing as well as the chartwork may be erased.

f The use of conventional symbols reduces the chance of a misunderstanding between different people using the chart. It also increases the chance of one person spotting another's errors.

There are reasons for the 'rules' but circumstances may arise in which common sense dictates that there are even better reasons for disregarding them.

6

a The Admiralty List of Lights is authoritative, comprehensive and can be kept up to date from Notices to Mariners. A yachtsman's almanac is re-issued each year and should be reasonably up to date, although it is not likely to be supported by a frequent issue of corrections. The specific information on lights which it contains is less detailed but it also contains a great deal of other information. It is therefore much cheaper and requires considerably less stowage space than a full set of Admiralty publications.

b Admiralty Sailing Directions are authoritative, comprehensive and are kept up to date by the periodic issue of supplements and new editions. However, they are intended for use by all vessels and much of the information they contain is therefore of little relevance to yachtsmen. Yachtsmen's sailing directions are written specifically for small craft and they contain very little information which is not directly relevant to yacht navigation. Admiralty Sailing Directions are intended to supplement charted information, whereas yachtsmen's sailing directions very often contain plans and sketch charts of harbours and anchorages so that they can be used instead of large-scale charts.

7 The Small Craft Edition of Admiralty Notices to Mariners NP 246, published four times each year, contains details of all changes to charted information which are considered essential to small craft navigating around the British Isles and Northwest Europe. Copies may be obtained from Admiralty Chart Agents, or as a subscription service through the RYA.

8 The Admiralty List of Radio Services for Small Craft, NP 280, published as a single volume. Corrections to radio information are published in both the Admiralty Notices to Mariners and the quarterly Small Craft Edition.

Exercise 2

1

a	Flashing every 10 seconds.	Fl 10 sec.	Fl 10s
b	Group flashing three every 15 seconds.	Gp Fl(3) 15 sec.	
		Fl(3) 15s	
c	Quick flashing.	Qk Fl.	Q
d	Isophase every 10 seconds.	Iso 10 sec.	Iso 10s
e	Occulting every 5 seconds.	Occ 5 sec.	Oc 5s
f	Alternating white red every 10 seconds.	Alt WR 10sec.	
		Al WR 10s	
g	Group occulting two every 20 seconds.	Gp Occ(2) 20sec.	
		Oc(2) 20s	

2

a Leave to port.
b Leave to starboard.
c Pass north of the buoy.
d Pass either side, preferably leaving it to port to keep to the starboard side of the channel.

3

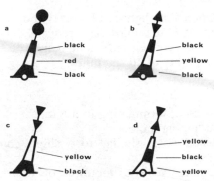

4

a Leave to starboard
b Pass south of the buoy
c Pass west of the buoy
d Leave to port

5 There is a possibility of a buoy dragging or parting its mooring and moving out of position. The possibility is remote with buoys marking major channels as they are carefully maintained and frequently checked. Because there are a limited number of distinguishing colours, shapes and topmarks available there is a chance of misidentifying a buoy, which must be guarded against.

6

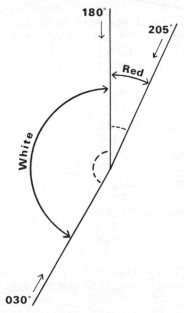

43

7 The focal plane of the light is 12 metres above the waterline and the nominal range is 24 sea miles. This range is the distance at which the light will be seen, given sufficient height of eye, by night, in meteorological visibility of 10 sea miles.

8

a Powerful low note, terminating in a 'grunt'.
b High-pitched 'piping' note.
c Medium pitched note, similar to a ship's compressed air fog signal.
d Low-pitched note. Whistles mounted on buoys tend to give an irregular pitch, low powered, sound.

Exercise 3

1	True course	125°(T)
	Variation	9°W
	Magnetic course	134°(M)

2	Magnetic course	240°(M)
	Variation	6°E
	True course	246°(T)

3		Lighthouse	Church	Windmill
	Magnetic bearings	022°(M)	066°(M)	138°(M)
	Variation	12°W	12°W	12°W
	True bearings	010°(T)	054°(T)	126°(T)

4	True course	310°(T)
	Variation	4°E
	Magnetic course	306°(M)
	Deviation	4°E
	Compass course	302°(C)

5	Compass course	170°(C)
	Deviation	7°W
	Magnetic course	163°(M)
	Variation	7°E
	True course	170°(T)

6 On course 125°(C) deviation is 5°W. Variation is 8°W. Total correction to convert compass to true bearings is therefore 13°W.

	Chimney	Beacon	Lighthouse
Compass bearings	207°(C)	245°(C)	303°(C)
Total corrections	13°W	13°W	13°W
True bearings	194°(T)	232°(T)	290°(T)

7 Total decrease in variation in 6 years is 48'. Correct variation to use is therefore 8° 22'W. In practice this should be rounded off to the nearest whole degree, and the variation to use is thus 8°W.

8 Charted transit of headland and lighthouse 339°(T)
Variation 8°W
Magnetic bearing 347°(M)
Observed compass bearing 342°(C)
Deviation is therefore 5°E
Total correction (variation and deviation combined) 3°W

Yacht's true course is 257°(T).

	Transit	Church	Flagstaff
Compass bearings	342°(C)	019°(C)	061°(C)
Total corrections	3°W	3°W	3°W
True bearings	339°(T)	016°(T)	058°(T)

9 The yacht must remain within 100 yards of the predetermined position to ensure that the error of the calculated bearing will be no more than ½°. (An angle of 1° subtends an arc of about 1 cable at 6 miles.)

Deviation Table

Ship's head (Compass)	Deviation	Ship's head (Compass)	Deviation
000°	2°E	180°	4°W
022½°	3½°E	202½°	5°W
045°	5°E	225°	6½°W
067½°	5°E	247½°	5½°W
090°	3°E	270°	4°W
112½°	1½°E	292½°	2°W
135°	0°	315°	½°W
157½°	2°W	337½°	½°E

Exercise 4 Answers

10 Compass course   040°(C)
     Deviation   2°E
     Magnetic course   042°(M)
     Heading by hand bearing compass   043°(C)
     Deviation of hand bearing compass   1°W

The deviation of the hand bearing compass will almost certainly be different if it is used in a different position in the yacht.

Exercise 4

1   Course   045°(C)
     Devn 2°E, Varn 6°W, Corrn   4°W
     Course steered   041°(T)
     Wake course   051°(T)
     Distance run 6.1−1.7 = 4.4M

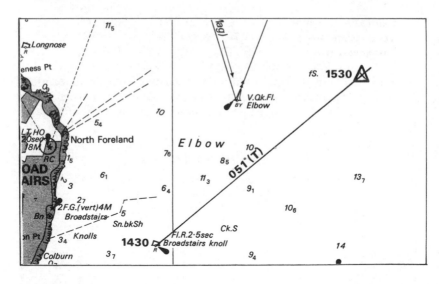

2   Course   255°(C)
     Devn 1°W, Varn 6°W, Corrn   7°W
     Course   248°(T)
     Distance run 21.5−18.4 = 3.1M
     Tidal set and drift 330°(T) 1.75M

     Course made good 275°(T).
     Distance run 3.7M, speed made good 4.8 knots.

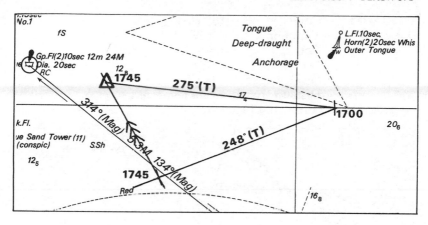

3 Course   245°(M)
      Variation   6°W
      Course   239°(T)
      Leeway   10°
      Wake course   249°(T)
      Distance run 88.0−83.2 = 4.8M
      Tidal set and drift 040°(T) 1.5M

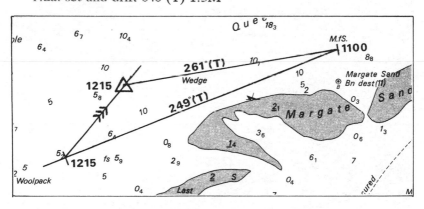

Course made good 261°(T).
Distance run 3.5M, speed made good 2.8 knots.

4 At 0830   Course   070°(M)
                    Variation   6°W
                    Course   064°(T)
                    Leeway   5°
                    Wake course   059°(T)
                    Distance run 14.0−11.7 = 2.3M

47

At 0855   Course   165°(M)
              Variation   6°W
              Course   159°(T)
              Leeway   5°
              Wake course   164°(T)
              Distance run 16.6−14.0 = 2.6M

Tidal set and drift 110°(T) 1.4M

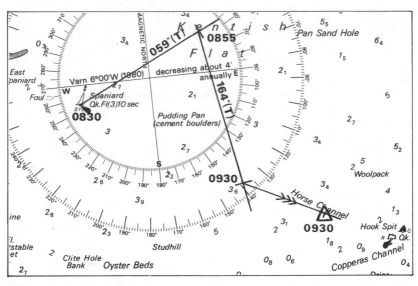

5   Course   114°(T)
                    Distance run   2.9M

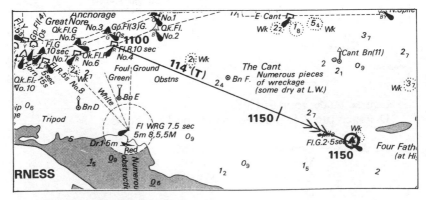

Tidal set and drift 110°(T) 1.3M.
Tidal stream has been 110°(T) 1.6 knots.

6 0640–0700 Wake course 119°(T), distance run 1.5M.
                 Tidal set and drift 080°(T) 0.8M.
   0700–0715 Wake course 119°(T), distance run 1.2M.
                 Tidal set and drift 110°(T) 0.5M.
   0715–0800 Wake course 009°(T), distance run 2.8M.
                 Tidal set and drift 110°(T) 1.5M.
   0800–0900 Wake course 354°(T), distance run 2.3M.
                 Tidal set and drift 190°(T) 1.1M.

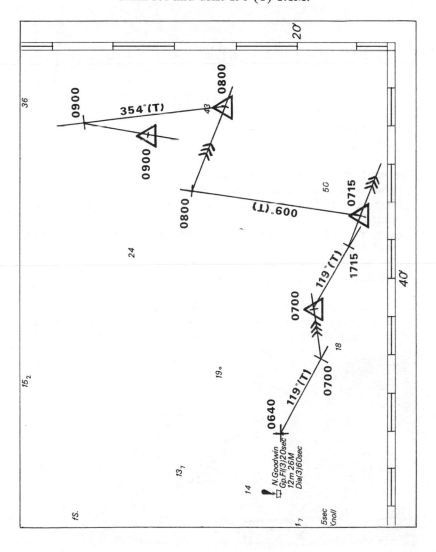

Exercise 5

1   The course to steer is 259°(T), speed made good 5.3 knots.

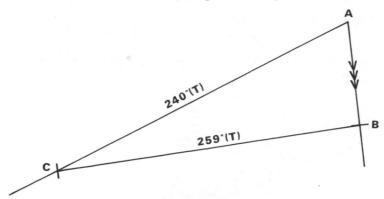

The method of working is as follows:
   From A, lay off the course to make good, 240°(T).
   From A, lay off the direction and rate of the tidal stream, to give point B.
   From B, strike an arc of radius 5 knots to cut the course to make good line at C.
   The direction B-C is the course to steer.
   The distance A-C is the speed made good.

2   The course to steer is 144°(T). The distance to go is 2.3 miles, speed made good 3.8 knots, so the time taken will be 36 minutes. The yacht will reach her destination at 0936.

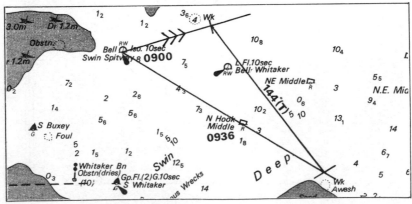

3 Steering one course to allow for the tidal stream throughout the leg results in the fastest passage. It is, of course, necessary to check that there is adequate sea room and that the yacht will not be set into danger during the passage.

4 The distance to go is about 6 sea miles so the time taken will be approximately 2 hours. The course to steer is 017°(T).

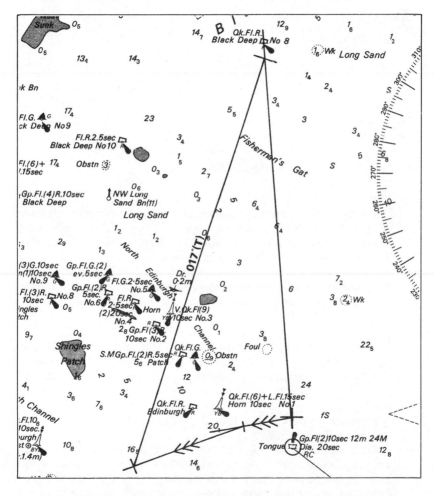

(The passage will in fact take slightly longer than the original approximation of 2 hours so for absolute accuracy the course to steer should be worked again. However, by making the second approximation the answer is unlikely to differ by more than ½°

51

and for all practical purposes the first approximation answer is perfectly accurate enough.)

5 Wake course required is 282°(T). Course to steer, allowing for leeway, is therefore 272°(T).

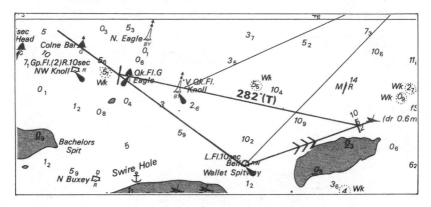

6 Distance to go is about 7½ sea miles and by inspection of the tidal streams the time taken will be approximately 3 hours. The wake course required is 266°(T); course to steer, allowing for leeway, 271°(T). The yacht will arrive at Girdler buoy at 1958.

The plot of positions at 1800 and 1900 shows that it is safe to steer a single course throughout the leg. *(See plot, page 53.)*

7 In this case there can be no question of steering a course to make good a particular direction because the yacht is hard on the wind. All the navigator can do is find out the course and speed she will make good on each tack and work out the time to put about for the buoy.

Heading on port tack will be 345°(T), wake course 350°(T) and course made good 008°(T).

Drawing in the lay line of 008°(T) to the SW Swin buoy and working out the course and speed made good from the SE Mouse buoy, it can be seen that the distance to go to the lay line is 2.6 sea miles and the speed made good is 3.1 knots. The time to tack is therefore 1551, when SW Swin buoy bears 008°(T).

The speed made good on the port tack will be 4.7 knots and the distance to sail is 2.6 sea miles. The yacht will therefore arrive at SW Swin buoy at 1624. *(See plot, page 54.)*

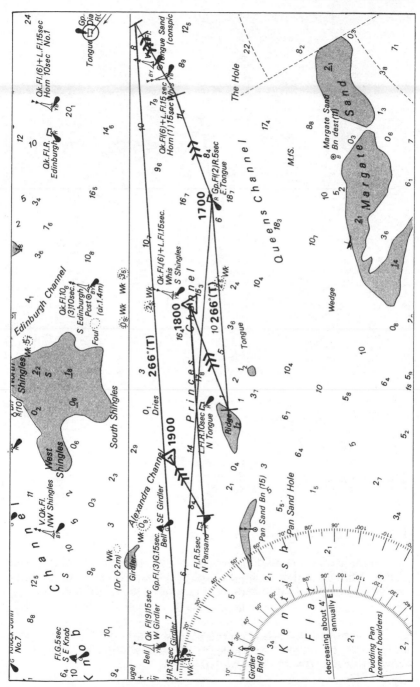

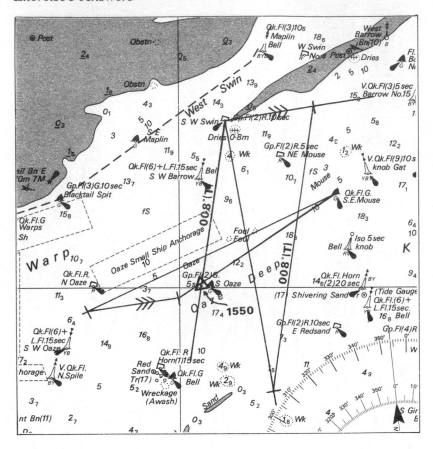

Exercise 6

1 See top of next page.

2 All three marks should be clearly and unambiguously charted and visible. They should be as close to the yacht as possible. The resulting position lines should intersect at angles of between 30° and 150°.

3
a Provided that it is steep-to it can be an excellent mark. If it is not steep-to the true edge may be below the horizon, or a drying area to seaward of the true edge may be visible.

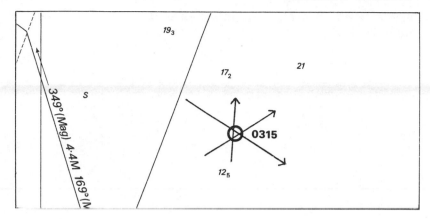

b A good mark, in the sense that it is positionally accurate, but it is unlikely to be visible at distances greater than about 1½ miles.

c Provided that it can be positively identified and there is no possibility of confusion with a neighbouring buoy with similar characteristics, it may be a useful mark. With any floating mark there is likely to be slight inaccuracy because of the scope of the cable and there is also the possibility of a floating mark dragging out of position.

d It is likely to be difficult to identify with certainty and unless the peak is very steep-sided its position will probably be rather vague.

e Buildings that are charted as conspicuous in the middle of towns very seldom are. A building which was conspicuous when the area was surveyed may become surrounded by similar developments, or even be dwarfed by higher ones.

f It can be surprisingly useful where a railway line runs along the foreshore, particularly on an unlit coast at night when the positions of the tunnel entrances can be identified as a train runs along the line. You need to be familiar with the coast to use them, however, to be sure that you are identifying tunnels rather than buildings or embankments on the seaward side of the line.

4 Any position fix should, as far as possible, be self-checking against gross error. By using three bearings any gross error, such as a bearing wrongly taken or plotted or a mark misidentified, should be revealed by the large 'cocked hat' in the resulting plot. It will be impossible to tell which bearing is wrong, simply that one of them is not correct and the fix should be re-taken.

5 The position line will be displaced 0.3 sea miles. (Each degree of

bearing error results in a positional error of 1/60th of the distance
from the mark)

6   The plot is:

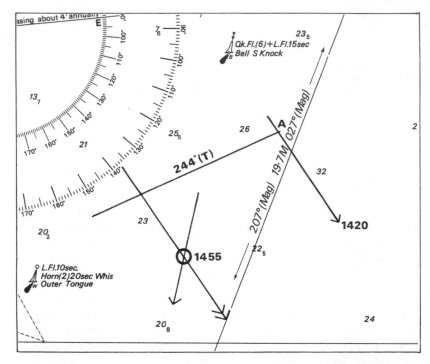

Position A is chosen arbitrarily as any point on the 1420 position line.
Your plot may therefore look different to the answer shown but the
resulting position should be the same.

7 The plot is:

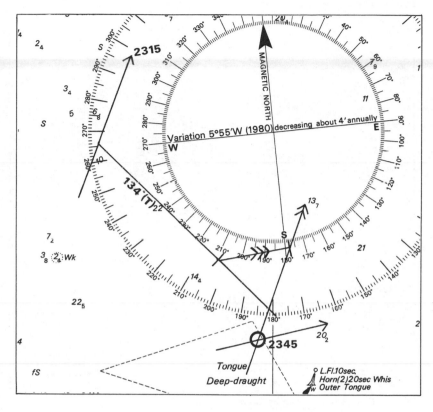

8 The plot is:

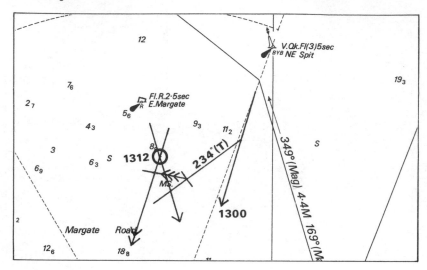

9 The plot is:

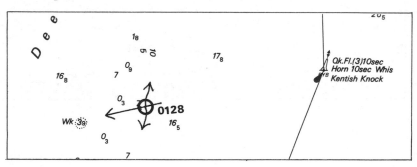

10 The plot is:

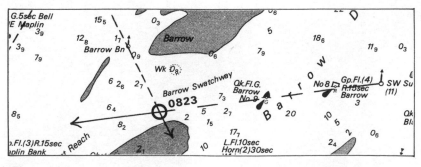

The fix should be reliable. The two transits are clearly defined and they have been confirmed by comparing the actual bearings with the charted bearings.

Exercise 7

1 Height of tide required is:
   Draft of yacht + Clearance − Charted depth
      1.8m   +   0.5   −   0.6m   = 1.7m

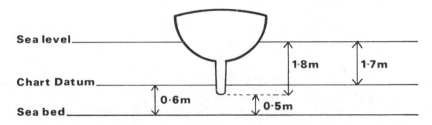

2 Height of tide will be :
   Draft of yacht + Charted drying height
      1.5m   +   1.2m   = 2.7m

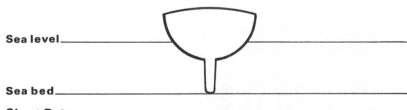

3 The height of the light is charted as 57m above MHWS.
   From the tidal differences table in the Data section, at Margate MHWS is 2.1m, Chart Datum−2.7m, so MHWS is 4.8m above Chart Datum. Height of tide is 2.7m below MHWS, so the light is 59.7m above sea level.

Exercise 7 Answers

4 From tide table for Harwich:

HW	2315		3.8m
DMR	0630	ML	2.2m
		HW−ML	1.6m
LW	1645		0.6m

5 From tide table for Sheerness:

HW	0741	4.7m
LW	0112	1.4m
	Range 3.3m	

Height required is 1.1m above LW.
Time at which it will reach this height is LW + 0225; i.e. 0337.

6 From tide table for Burnham-on-Crouch:

HW	1859	4.6m
	ML	3.0m
	HW −ML	1.6m
	LW	1.4m
	Range 3.2m	

Height required is 0.8m below high water.
Time at which it will reach this height is HW−0155, i.e. 1704.

7 From tide table for Dover:

HW	1649	5.9m
LW	1131	1.9m
	Range 4.0m	

Time required is LW + 0230.
Height above LW will be 1.5m.
Height of tide will be 3.4m.

8 From tide table for Harwich:

HW	1931	3.5m
ML		2.2m
HW−ML		1.3m
LW		0.9m Range 2.6m

Time required is HW + 0130.
Fall from HW will be 0.4m.
Height of tide will be 3.1m.

9 Standard port from which to work is Dover.

At Dover	HW	0326	6.3m	and	1546
Corrns for Ramsgate		+0020	−1.6m		+0020
At Ramsgate		0346	4.7m		1606
ML			2.6m	DMR	0530
HW−ML			2.1m		
LW			0.5m		1136

At Ramsgate, HW 0346, 4.7m; LW 1136, 0.5m.

10 Standard port from which to work is Harwich.

At Harwich	HW	2032	3.2m
Corrections		−0025	−0.8m
At Orford Haven		2007	2.4m
DMR		0640ML	1.8m
	HW−ML		0.6m
LW		1327	1.2m

At Orford Haven Bar, HW 2007, 2.4m; LW 1327, 1.2m.

11 It is likely that high waters will exceed paredicted heights and levels will not fall as low as predicted at low waters. There is also a possiblity that both high and low waters will occur later than predicted. This answer is based on the general premise that stronge onshore winds and a low barometer will both tend to raise predicted levels rather than on any unique feature of the Thames Estuary.

12

a The tidal stream atlas presents information in a form in which it is very easy to assimilate and use. Each page gives a good general impression of the direction and rate of flow and specific details for a particular position are quite easy to extract. For ease of reference pages can be labelled with the dates and times to which they apply.

b Tidal diamonds on charts provide extremely accurate information on the streams in the positions to which they relate. They do not have the same visual impact as the tidal stream atlas and the coverage of areas for which they are available is rather limited. They are particularly useful as an indication of directions and rates in harbour entrances.

c Tidal stream notes in sailing directions are particularly useful for drawing attention to features which cannot be illustrated in atlases or tidal diamonds. Phenomena such as local eddies of limited extent and areas where dangerous overfalls or turbulence occur at certain states of the tide are described, although not necessarily quantified.

Exercise 8

1

Shelter   Under this heading should be considered the effectiveness of shelter from the present wind and sea and any changes in direction which might be expected to occur. Shelter from the tidal stream must also be considered: in extreme cases one would not wish to risk dragging because of a very fast stream, and if it is intended to go ashore in the tender it is desirable not to have to battle aginst a fast stream.

Holding ground   Clay, mud and sand are good; broken shells, shingle and gravel might be considered adequate in light winds and weak tidal streams. Rock is poor, and a heavy growth of weed is likely to prevent the anchor digging into the sea bed below it. Care must also be taken to avoid submarine cables and mooring ground chains.

Depth of water and range of tide   It must be no deeper at high water than one-third of the available length of cable if anchoring with chain or one-fifth of the length of cable if anchoring with warp. Except in the case of a bilge-keeler or if using legs, it must be deep enough to remain afloat at low water. If it is intended to dry out at low water it is important to be certain that the sea bed is reasonably firm and level; it is possible for a bilge-keeler to roll over if she grounds with one keel on the edge of a trench.

Swinging room   This may be obstructed by shoal water, moorings or other boats at anchor. It may be perfectly safe to anchor quite close to another yacht with a similar underwater shape because she will have a similar response to the influence of wind and stream. However it is anti-social, if not actually dangerous, to obstruct the swinging circle of a yacht already at anchor.

Navigational access   It must be possible to navigate safely to the chosen berth. Ideally, unless the berth is well sheltered from all quarters it should also be possible to leave it at any state of the tide, by day or night, if a change in the weather makes it necessary to clear out.

Fairways, ferry routes and busy channels   It is important not to obstruct a fairway when anchoring. It is also a good idea to avoid areas close to routes used by ferries, tripper boats and other large craft whose wash would make life uncomfortable.

Proximity of a landing place   As one of the reasons for anchoring is likely to be to go ashore, the berth should be as close as possible to a safe landing place.

Non-navigational criteria   Other aspects, such as scenic attraction and seclusion, may well be the prime reasons for visiting a particular anchorage.

2   There is a lack of detailed information about depths on the chart but if you do not cross the drying line you should have sufficient depth of water. (The legend 'Dries', close south of Whitstable Street N cardinal buoy, looks like cryptic cartography; it does not appear to relate to any particular charted feature.)

The echosounder will not necessarily give any warning if you are too far inshore as you approach the drying part of Whitstable Street. A useful clearing line, given good visibility, is the seaward end of Herne Bay Pier in transit with Reculvers (North Tower). By keeping north of this line you will clear the northern end of Whitstable Street. An alternative is the yellow sewer outfall buoy in transit with the end of Herne Bay Pier: it leads slightly further to seaward but the marks are closer and less likely to become invisible at the crucial moment.

Approaching the entrance to the Swale, the transit of Pollard Spit buoy with the wind pump north of Shell Ness gives a clearing line for the shallow water off Whitstable Flats.

It would also be worth keeping an eye on the echosounder: if the depth shoals to 2m you are too far south and need to make some ground to the north.

3   The only underwater obstructions shown on the chart are two sewer outfalls marked by buoys and the groynes off Frinton. It should be safe to use the echosounder to give a clearing line for the ends of the inshore tacks, going about when the depth is 2.5m. After passing the sewer outfall buoy off Frinton the clearing depth should be increased to 3m to give positive clearance off the ends of the groynes, unless you find that these are marked by beacons.

4   No. This is the classic trap for anyone placing too much reliance on soundings. If you simply sail by the sounder you are likely to stand inside the spit, marked as 'Numerous obstructions in the area', at Maplin Edge and ground on the spit after tacking onto starboard.

5   On the leg between Red Sand and SW Barrow the skipper gave the helmsman a mark to steer for. Throughout this leg the yacht was being set to the west and instead of following a track of about 010°(T) she followed a curve of pursuit, arriving at SW Barrow on a heading of about 080°(T). The next buoy which the helmsman sighted ahead was therefore NE Mouse, not SW Swin. The characteristics of the two are identical but the period, which the skipper did not mention so the helmsman could not check, is different.

The next mark which the helmsman picked up was Barrow No 15, with a characteristic very similar to Maplin, which the skipper thought he was heading for. Finally the helmsman sighted Barrow No. 12, the characteristic of which differs sufficiently from Maplin Bank for him to alert the skipper to the fact that all was not well.

Four navigational errors contributed to this fiasco. The helmsman was never given a compass course to steer so he was unaware that his heading differed considerably from that which his skipper intended. The periods of the lights were not checked. No check was made on any navigational mark other than the one which was assumed to be the next ahead. The skipper tried to navigate the chart table rather than the yacht, thus isolating himself from the reality of what was going on around him.

6 Withies are branches of trees. They are less substantial than most navigational marks and are easily knocked down or swept away. As they are often put in position and maintained by volunteers rather than a harbour authority it would be over-optimistic to rely on them implicitly.

Many of the channels marked by withies dry out or carry very little depth at low water so it would be wrong to assume that it is necessarily safe to navigate between them. They mark, in a relative sense, the deeper water; it might be safer to regard them as marking the less shallow water.

If a channel marked by withies carries a navigable depth at all states of the tide it is quite likely that the withies themselves will be placed on the drying side of the low water mark. They should be given a reasonably wide berth.

7 In strong onshore winds or an onshore swell there are likely to be dangerous breaking waves on a bar. The shallower the water the greater the possibility of dangerous conditions and the danger is likely to be greater with an ebb stream running out towards the seas than with a flood.

8 *Skipper steering* The advantage is that the skipper can react instantly if things go wrong and he can steer exactly the course he wants. The disadvantage is that he can spend very little time studying the chart or picking out marks ahead. With a well thought out, simple, navigational plan the method can work well, particularly if the skipper has developed the ability to memorise much of the detail of the chart.

Crew member steering Problems most often arise with this method because of difficulties of communication. The skipper must be unambiguous in his instructions. A request to steer 'A little to port' is unlikely to be interpreted exactly as it was intended. How much is a little?

There are three ways in which the skipper may give steering instructions so that they are absolutely clear:

a By using compass courses. Ideally these should be pre-planned but this is not absolutely essential; the helmsman can be given the course to steer as soon as the skipper is happy that the yacht is on the right heading.

b By reference to marks ahead, either steering directly towards something or between two buoys. The possible danger is that a cross-tide may carry the yacht out of the channel so that she grounds even when still heading for the correct mark.

c By using transits. This is the ideal method and it does not necessarily need special marks. As long as there is some perspective to the scenery ahead it should nearly always be possible to pick out a natural transit.

The great advantage of having a crew member on the helm is that it leaves the skipper free to concentrate on the navigation. It also makes harbour entries more interesting for the crew.

9 Prepare an anchor for letting go and make sure that the cable is clear to run. If anything goes wrong during the passage up the channel you may need to anchor very quickly.

Consider changing down to a smaller headsail. There might be three advantages in doing so: a smaller sail, cut high at the clew, would improve visibility forward, it would be quicker and easier to tack, and it would keep the speed a little slower. Avoid any temptation to reduce sail so much that the yacht barely has steerage way.

Check that all sheets and halyards are clear to run and that the cockpit and working areas on deck are clear and unobstructed. If there is a spray hood over the hatch, consider lowering it to improve visibility.

If using a towed log, hand it.

Switch on the echosounder to check that it is working.

If you are going to pick up a buoy, check that the boathook and a picking-up line are to hand. If you are going to an alongside berth make sure that warps and fenders can be made ready without having to empty the entire contents of a deep locker onto the cockpit sole.

Exercise 9

1

a *Tidal heights* These are likely to be a dominant factor in any passage plan in areas where there are drying harbours or drying bars. Clearly the plan must ensure that there is sufficient height of tide to give an adequate safety margin when entering and leaving harbour or crossing shallows.

There may also be occasions when it is desirable to make part of a passage close to low water. For instance, where there is an unmarked channel through mud flats it may be relatively simple to follow the line of the deep water when the banks on either side are uncovered. At high water the whole area may appear a featureless expanse of water, with a foot of water covering the banks and nothing to indicate the line of the channel.

For exploring poorly marked channels a rising tide is almost essential. Touching a sandy or muddy bottom as the tide rises is a reasonable way of finding where the shallow water is: grounding in a remote place on a falling tide is always tedious and sometimes dangerous.

b Tidal streams On a coastal passage tidal streams are very often the most important factor to be considered in deciding the best time to sail. In areas where the streams run at over 3 knots it is reasonable to expect to make 30-40 miles on one favourable tide, but in the following six hours one might be lucky to make 10 miles over the ground against the foul stream.

Where there are very strong streams, running at anything up to 8 knots round prominent headlands or through narrow gullies, it will probably be essential to arrive at the areas of fastest streams within about half an hour of slack water in order to avoid dangerous overfalls.

c Time of day There are some skippers and crews who cannot face life until after a large, late breakfast. For them, time of day is all-important in deciding when to put to sea.

For everyone, the position of the sun can make all the difference between simple and very difficult navigation. Entering an unfamiliar harbour with small, inconspicuous or distant leading marks is much easier with the light behind you than with a low morning or evening sun shining straight in your eyes. Good sunglasses help to overcome the problem but a coastline tends to look dull, flat and featureless when seen against the light. With the sun high in the sky or shining from seaward the scene comes to life and the landmarks stand out clearly.

d Hours of daylight/darkness Some passages are impossible in the dark; there just aren't enough lights to make navigation possible. There are also times when darkness can be a help. Making a landfall on an unfamiliar coast, for instance, the lights are often easier to identify by their characteristics and periods by night than are the salient features of the land by day. An hour or so before dawn is a favourite time to make a landfall; the yacht's position can be established from bearings of the lights and there is daylight for entering harbour..

e Forecast wind direction and strength If comfortable sailing rather than a particular destination was the aim of a cruise and time was not limited it would be very pleasant always to sail downwind. However, if a skipper is determined to go to a particular destination he has to take the wind very much as he finds it. He may be able to gain some shelter and smooth water from a weather shore, and safety demands the lee shores should be given a wide berth. If two different routes are available it will be prudent to choose the windward one rather than give ground to leeward.

Wind strength is the factor which determines whether or not a passage is safe. It is impossible to be dogmatic about forecasts which should keep a yacht in harbour; it all depends on the strength of the boat and her crew, the shelter, or lack of it, other aspects of the weather such as the visibility, and the extent to which the crew enjoy rough weather.

f Ranges of navigational lights There is little point in planning a passage along the coast just out of sight of the lights; much better to make a short dog-leg so that lights are visible for fixing.

g Phase of the moon A full moon, even through quite thick cloud, gives a very useful light. An unlit creek may be easily navigable at night with a full moon but impossible between dusk and dawn without one.

h Traffic separation schemes Traffic separation schemes dictate the course of every vessel navigating in them, by force of law. Strictly speaking a yacht on passage along a scheme should navigate in the traffic lane designated for vessels travelling in her direction. In practice it is more sensible to keep clear of the lanes and make the passage through an inshore zone to the side of the scheme. Yachts must not navigate in a lane against the direction of traffic flow.

If it is necessary to cross a traffic separation scheme, it must be crossed as nearly as practicable at right angles.

2

a North Edinburgh Channel route This channel is deep and closely buoyed, indicating that it is the main big-ship channel to the Thames and Medway ports. It is therefore an area to avoid, if possible, although by keeping to the shallow water side of the buoys a yacht can navigate it without in any way impeding ships confined to the channel. From the inner end of the Edinburgh there is a hitch to the north, with the stream on the starboard bow to slow progress before turning west with the stream on the quarter round the north of East Barrow Sand.

The route is certainly navigable: the main point against it is the proximity to the busy shipping channel.

b South Edinburgh Channel route The South Edinburgh is sparsely buoyed so although it carries a reasonable depth of water it does not look like a major shipping route. However, after leaving the South Edinburgh there is a very busy highway to cross in the Knob and Knock John channels. From Mid Barrow to South Whitaker there will be a contrary stream to punch.

Again, a possible route but with even less to recommend it than (a), in view of the shipping lanes to cross and the length of the leg against the stream.

c Fisherman's Gat route This is the 'country lane' route; it avoids the likelihood of encounters with ships in narrow channels which are the main drawbacks of both (a) and (b). Again there is some ground to make against the stream but it is a relatively short leg. More of the passage is in open water, with plenty of sea room.

Fisherman's Gat looks the best bet.

3

a The planned route This passage should be no more difficult by night than by day. There is a favourable stream for the next four hours and with luck it should be possible to make Sheerness before there is any weight of ebb stream running.

The vital buoys, SE Margate, S Margate, E Last and Spaniard, should be easy to pick out as there will be no shore lights behind them and there will always be a light visible ahead or astern to show the line of the channel.

b Queen's Channel route There is certainly more sea room in the Queen's Channel. It adds about 4 miles to the distance to sail and takes the yacht into rougher water away from the lee of the land; it also entails giving away ground to leeward which is seldom a sensible thing to do. The route has very little to recommend it.

c Anchor off Margate Why waste a favourable tide and useful breeze? The pubs closed an hour and a half ago.

4 The passage will only be possible after the wind has veered and moderated.

The distance from Deben Bar to the entrance to the Swale is about 40 miles, a distance which it should be possible to cover in eight hours with a fair wind and favourable stream.

The tides predicted for Thursday 6 August are:

	HW		LW		HW	
Sheerness	0528	5.4m	1049	1.1m	1740	5.3m
Harwich	0446	3.7m	1027	0.7m	1657	3.7m
Deben Bar	0431	3.3m	1007	0.7m	1642	3.3m
Dover	0343	6.0m	1100	1.6m	1601	6.2m

The tidal stream off the Deben will be setting to the northeast until about 1025 and then to the southwest. The favourable stream for the passage will continue until about 1800.

There will be insufficient depth to sail from the Deben within 2½ hours of low water: according to the tide table the bar is awash at chart datum. Before 0730 and after 1230 there will be sufficient depth to give 0.5m clearance. If sailing is dealyed until 1230 the last few hours of the passage will be against the full run of the ebb. It would be preferable to accept some foul stream at the start of the passage where the rates are not so strong.

Provided that the wind has moderated and veered by the morning it would be best to plan on sailing at 0700 to be clear of the bar by 0730. If the wind is still very strong and south of west then, sailing should be delayed until 1230, to make the first part of the passage, as far as the Rivers Colne or Crouch, anchoring there to wait for the next favourable tide. (It might be possible to sail shortly after midnight to take the earlier tide to the Colne or the Crouch if the wind veers and decreases very early but there would not be a great deal to be gained by doing so.)

The most promising route for the passage is round the Naze, up the Wallet to the Spitway, across the mouth of the Crouch to the West Swin, and across the Oaze to approach the Swale from the north. This route keeps as close as possible under the lee of the land and although it may give slightly less fair tide than going outside the Gunfleet and up Barrow Deep, the shelter of the land is likely to be the more useful bonus to a small shallow draft yacht.

You should arrive at the Spitway at about the time of low water but there will be 2m depth of water (this is the shallowest part of the route). You should be off the mouth of the Swale by 1600. In the event of the wind falling light you will need to keep a close eye on the time and distance to go, if necessary motoring in order to arrive off the Swale by 1800. If you are much later than this you may have a very long slog against the strengthening ebb.

Exercise 10

1   The estimated position cannot be relied on after 12 hours without a fix. The echosounder should be running to give warning of shallow water. The three radio beacons on the chart, Sunk, Tongue and North Foreland, are all a long way away but it would be worth trying to obtain bearings of them, at least to confirm that the EP is not substantially in error. As soon as it is possible to pick up the signal from Sunk it should be possible to home in on the light vessel from a safe bearing and establish the yacht's exact position.

2   The radio beacon is the Sunk Light Vessel, with a stated range of 10 miles. The bearing must be 245°(M), 239°(T), as the depth indicates that the yacht cannot be to the west of the light vessel. It is very difficult to estimate the distance from the radio beacon; the signal strength depends as much on radio propagation conditions and the sensitivity of the receiver as on the transmitted signal strength. However the range is not important in order to work out the course to steer. The tidal stream for the next few hours will be setting about 190°(T) at 2 knots, so the course to steer is 261°(T), 267°(M). (See the plot in the answer to Question 3. In this plot a starting point has been chosen as the closest point along the 0905 position line to the 0900 EP. This is simply a convenient point to plot from; it is not intended to imply that the yacht is in this position at 0905.

3   The radio beacons are Sunk, Tongue and North Foreland. Tongue can be identified by its frequency and time of transmission.

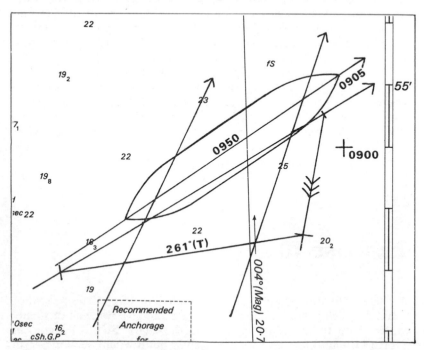

The discrepancy between the bearings from Tongue and North Foreland is not unduly large; it represents inaccuracies in each bearing of a little over 1°. There is now an indication that the yacht is probably somewhere within the lozenge shown on the plot. It is useful to note that the radio bearings show a measure of agreement with the depth by echosounder.

4 The course to make good is 280°(T), distance to go 7.1M. The predicted tidal streams are, approximately:

> 1100–1200   215°(T) 2 knots
> 1200–1300   235°(T) 1 knot

By inspection, the passage will take about 1½ hours.

From the plot in the answer to question 5, course to steer is 308°(M). The assumption of 1½ hours for the passage is not quite accurate, but any error will tend to take the yacht up-tide of her destination and thus it will be easy to correct.

5 The course steered is 304°(T), distance run 2.0M, estimated set and drift 215°(T) 1.0M. *(See next page)*

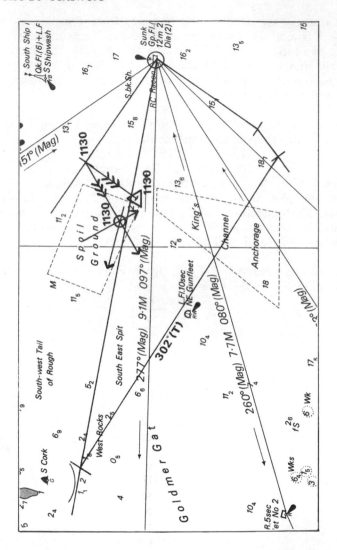

The actual set and drift has been 243°(T) 1.0M, so the tidal stream has been 243°(T) 2 knots.

6 Depart from Heaps buoy closehauled on starboard tack, steering 010°(T). The course made good will be 026°(T), speed made good 5.5 knots. Predicted tidal stream is 060° 2 knots.

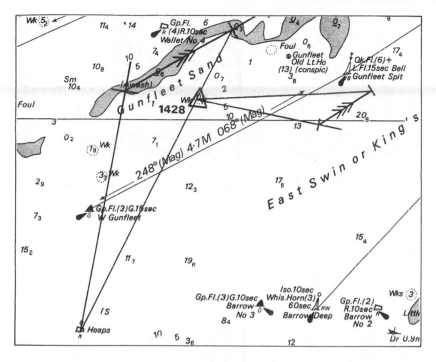

Watch the echosounder carefully to pick up the 10m depth contour (expected at 1521, log reading 12.2), and the 5m depth contour (expected at 1528, log reading 12.9).

The nearest point for which there is tidal height information is Walton on the Naze, standard port Harwich:

Harwich   HW 1317   4.0m
Walton   HW 1307   4.1m   LW 0.3m   Range 3.8m
Heights for Walton   1407   3.8m, 1507 3.2m, 1607 2.2m.

These heights should be plotted and a graph drawn to give the correction to add to charted depth to compare with the depth by echosounder at any time.

At the 5m depth contour line tack onto port, steering 100°(T), making good 086°(T). The echosounder should now show deepening water. Coninue past the 10m depth contour line for 5 minutes and then tack back onto starboard. Stand in to the 5m depth contour, taking great care not to cross it, and repeat the process. It should be impossible to sail between Gunfleet Spit buoy and the sand without sighting the buoy, or to sail far enough to seaward to pass south of it without a sighting. If you do sail slightly too far to the north you should see Gunfleet Old Light House before you are in any danger of being caught by the hook of drying sand.

A good lookout, by sight and sound will be needed throughout this leg, both for shipping and navigational marks.

The steeply shelving south side of the Gunfleet gives a useful line to Gunfleet Spit buoy, making the approach from the west the most attractive option in these circumstances. It might be possible to work the leg in other ways, leaving Heaps buoy on port tack and using the depth contours around the east end of NE Middle to give a lead to Barrow No. 3 buoy. It should then be possible to lay Gunfleet Spit on starboard, but if the buoy does not appear when expected it would be a toss up to decide which way to turn to look for it.

Other Stanford Maritime books on navigation, seamanship and cruising

Navigation for Yachtsmen   *Mary Blewitt*
Coastwise Navigation   *Gordon Watkins*
Exercises in Coastal Navigation   *G.W. White*
Celestial Navigation for Yachtsmen   *Mary Blewitt*
Exercises in Astro-navigation   *Gordon Watkins*
Basic Principles of Marine Navigation   *D.A. Moore*
Marine Chartwork 2nd edition   *D.A. Moore*
Traverse and Other Tables   Burton's Nautical Tables
Planispheres   Stars at a Glance
Outlook: Weather Maps and Elementary Forecasting
    G.W. White
Meteorology for Yachtsmen*   *Ray Sanderson*
International Light, Shape and Sound Signals   *D.A. Moore*
Guide to the Collision Avoidance Rules
    Cockcroft & Lameijer
✳Stanford's Sailing Companion 4th edition ✳
    Capt. R.J.F. Riley
Stanford's Tidal Atlases   *Michael Reeve-Fowkes*
Norwegian Cruising Guide   *Mark Brackenbury*
Baltic Pilot*   *Mark Brackenbury*
Frisian Pilot   *Mark Brackenbury*
Barge Country–the Netherlands Waterways   *John Liley*
France–the Quiet Way   *John Liley*
Brittany and Channel Islands Cruising Guide   *David Jefferson*
Scottish West Coast Pilot   *Mark Brackenbury*
Shell Encyclopedia of Sailing   *ed. Michael Richey*
Practical Yacht Handling   *Eric Tabarly*
Motorboat & Yachting Manual 19th edition*   *Dick Hewitt*
After 50,000 Miles   *Hal Roth*
Capsize in a Trimaran   *Nicolas Angel*
Better Boat Handling*   *Des Sleightholme*
Race Navigation*   *Stuart Quarrie*

*In preparation at the time of publication of this book

For a complete list of nautical books and charts, write to the Sales Manager, Stanford
Maritime Ltd, 12–14 Long Acre, London WC2E 9LP